BATTLEFIELDS ACROSS AMERICA

LITTLE BIGHORN

RANDY KREHBIEL

Twenty-First Century Books

A Division of Henry Holt and Company

New York

Twenty-First Century Books
A Division of Henry Holt and Company, Inc.
115 West 18th Street
New York, New York 10011

Henry Holt® and colophon are registered trademarks of Henry Holt and
Company, Inc.
Publishers since 1866

Published in Canada by Fitzhenry & Whiteside Ltd.
195 Allstate Parkway, Markham, Ontario L3R 4T8

Printed in the United States of America on acid free paper ∞.

Created and produced in association with Blackbirch Graphics, Inc.

Photo Credits
Cover: © Travel Montana/Department of Commerce/Donnie Sexton; pages 4, 8,
13, 18, 37, 38 (top), 38 (bottom), 41, 51: North Wind Pictures; pages 10, 15, 21
(top), 21 (bottom), 23, 28, 30, 34, 45, 46: Courtesy Little Bighorn National
Monument; pages 48, 53 (top left): © John Kwapinski/Fort Ransom State Park;
page 50, 53 (top right), 53 (bottom): Travel Montana/Department of Commerce;
page 54: © Robb DeWall/Crazy Horse Memorial Foundation.
All maps by Bob Italiano/© Blackbirch Press, Inc.

Library of Congress Cataloging-in-Publication Data

Krehbiel, Randy.
    Little Bighorn / Randy Krehbiel.—1st ed.
        p.   cm.—(Battlefields across America)
    Includes bibliographical references and index.
    Summary: Chronicles the Indian Wars with a focus on the Battle of Little Bighorn
and the career of George Armstrong Custer.
    ISBN 0-8050-5236-4 (alk. paper)
    1. Little Bighorn, Battle of the, Mont., 1876—Juvenile literature. 2. Custer, George
Armstrong, 1839-1876—Juvenile literature. [1. Little Bighorn, Battle of the, Mont.,
1876. 2. Custer, George Armstrong, 1839-1876.] I. Title. II. Series.
E83.876.K74 1997
973.8′2—dc21   97-29420
                                                                                   CIP
                                                                                    AC

CONTENTS

P A R T   O N E

THE 400-YEAR FIGHT FOR AMERICA

From the moment Europeans and American Indians first met there was conflict. Neither knew much about the other and both were unsure how to react. They were unaccustomed to each other's ways. Often friends as well as foes, they fought both for and against each other for nearly four centuries.

What they were fighting for was North America. The Indian nations, numbering in the hundreds, had lived in the Americas for thousands of years before the Europeans arrived. The Indians knew the valleys, mountains, rivers, and plains of North America. They had distinctive ways of life suited to their surroundings. This had been the Indians' land to live on freely, but they were no match for the waves of settlers that began arriving after 1500.

The newcomers were aggressive, well armed, and well organized. In addition, the Europeans brought with them diseases, such as smallpox, for which the Indian population had no immunity. These diseases killed hundreds of thousands of Indians, often wiping out entire villages.

The Indians who resisted the onslaught of Europeans arriving in North America did so bravely. In 1622 and 1644, for example, the Powhatan Confederation defended their territory against the Virginia colonists. Northeastern tribes inflicted great harm on New England settlements in 1675-76, and in 1680, the Pueblo chased the Spanish from present-day New Mexico. In 1791, an army of Miami, Shawnee, and other tribes killed and wounded more than 900 soldiers under General Arthur St. Clair near what is now Fort Wayne, Indiana. St. Clair, a Revolutionary War officer, had been sent to stop Indian raids on the new white settlements north of the Ohio River.

< 5 >

< 6 >

The Indian victories, however, were usually followed by defeat. The white newcomers, sometimes with help from Indian allies, always regrouped and came back with bigger armies and more powerful weapons. And, as the United States became a stronger nation, the Indians found themselves in an impossible position. No matter which side they chose—fighting for or against the whites—the results were the same: loss of life, loss of land, and ultimately, loss of identity. By the end of the Civil War, in 1865, few Indian groups remained east of the Mississippi River.

Many Indian nations disappeared entirely, having been wiped out by war or disease, or absorbed into other tribes. Some tribes moved westward. Eventually, however, the new Americans began moving west as well.

The coming of railroads and the passage of legislation such as the 1862 Homestead Act sent white settlers flooding into remote parts of the country. The semi-nomadic Indians of the northern Plains needed open space and undisturbed hunting grounds. They soon felt cramped by the surge in population.

Skirmishes became more frequent and further strained relations between the Indians and the whites. In 1864, volunteers under Colonel John Chivington attacked a Cheyenne village at Sand Creek, Colorado. The village leader, Chief Black Kettle, wanted to maintain peaceful relations with the United States and so had moved his people to Sand Creek at the army's urging. Chivington's men, however, killed every Indian in sight. This unprovoked slaughter destroyed what little trust the Plains tribes still had in the army and any hopes that the army would deal fairly with them. Another incident, which occurred ten years earlier in 1854, can now be seen as an indicator of the events that were to come. A Miniconjou Lakota Sioux named High Forehead shot a lame cow that belonged to a Mormon wagon train on the Oregon Trail. As a result, a hotheaded U.S. Army

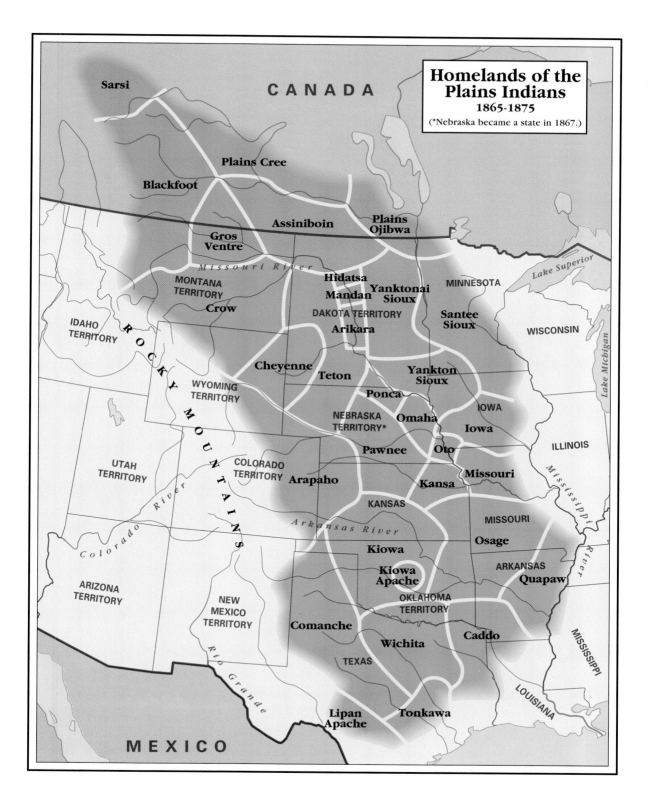

Homelands of the Plains Indians
1865-1875
(*Nebraska became a state in 1867.)

Sarsi

CANADA

Plains Cree

Blackfoot

Assiniboin

Plains Ojibwa

Gros Ventre

Missouri River

MONTANA TERRITORY

Crow

Hidatsa

Mandan

Yanktonai Sioux

MINNESOTA

Lake Superior

DAKOTA TERRITORY

Arikara

Santee Sioux

WISCONSIN

IDAHO TERRITORY

R O C K Y   M O U N T A I N S

Cheyenne

Teton

Yankton Sioux

Lake Michigan

WYOMING TERRITORY

Ponca

Omaha

IOWA

NEBRASKA TERRITORY*

Iowa

Oto

ILLINOIS

UTAH TERRITORY

Colorado River

COLORADO TERRITORY

Arapaho

Pawnee

Kansa

Missouri

Mississippi River

KANSAS

Arkansas River

MISSOURI

Osage

ARIZONA TERRITORY

NEW MEXICO TERRITORY

Kiowa

Kiowa Apache

ARKANSAS

Quapaw

OKLAHOMA TERRITORY

MISSISSIPPI

Comanche

Wichita

Caddo

Rio Grande

TEXAS

LOUISIANA

Lipan Apache

Tonkawa

MEXICO

Tensions between Plains Indians and white settlers grew as westward expansion threatened Indian territory.

lieutenant named John Grattan was sent from Fort Laramie, Wyoming, with a small group of men to arrest High Forehead. Grattan became violent and fired his two cannons at the Indians. In defense, the Indians killed Grattan along with the rest of his men.

A young Oglala Lakota Sioux boy known as Curly witnessed this violent outburst and was deeply affected by it. Twelve years later, then answering to the name Crazy Horse, he would fight against the whites in the Powder River War.

The Powder River War

The Powder River War was fought over possession of the Bozeman Trail, which was a shortcut from Fort Laramie in southeastern Wyoming to the gold fields of southwest Montana. A string of U.S. Army forts had been built along the trail in the Powder River country of northern Wyoming. In objection to these forts, under the leadership of the chief Red Cloud, the Brule, Oglala, and Miniconjou

< 9 >

Lakota (all Sioux subtribes), and their friends the northern Cheyenne kept the Bozeman Trail closed for two years. In 1868, the U.S. government abandoned the Powder River forts, and in the Treaty of 1868 declared the western half of present-day South Dakota a Sioux reservation. (A reservation is a parcel of land set aside by the U.S. government for a group of Indians to live on.) This reservation included the Black Hills—called the *Paha Sapa* by the Lakota Sioux. Furthermore, the Sioux were allowed to roam a loosely defined area in eastern Montana called the "unceded territory."

The Sioux believed that they had won a great victory. In reality, however, they had only won a little time. William Tecumseh Sherman, a famous Civil War general, was the military commander of the Plains at the time when the Treaty of 1868 was signed. Although the treaty had been a victory of sorts for the Indians in the north, Sherman turned his Army's attention southward.

The commanding officer on the southern Plains was General Phil Sheridan, Sherman's trusted Civil War comrade. Together, the two men intended to wage what they called "total war" against the Indians, just as they had done against the Confederate South.

Custer and the Battle of the Washita

Later in 1868, Sheridan brought Lieutenant Colonel George Armstrong Custer to the Plains. Another Civil War hero, Custer's job was to track down and punish Indian parties that had been conducting raids into Kansas. Although it was November, Sheridan believed that winter was the best time to attack. During the spring and summer, the Indians were scattered in small bands that were almost impossible to find and even harder to pin down. In winter, the bands came together to form large, semi-permanent villages. These were easier for the soldiers to attack. Riding through

Under Custer's command, the army killed innocent Indians during the battle of the Washita.

a blizzard, and in subzero temperatures, Custer and his Seventh Cavalry tracked a band of Cheyenne deep into Indian Territory— now western Oklahoma. On the night of November 26, the soldiers stumbled upon a large camp along the Washita River—where Black Kettle was living after Sand Creek.

Despite the slaughter at Sand Creek, Black Kettle still sought peace with the whites. Only days before Custer's men found his village, Black Kettle told other army officers he wanted no part of war. Custer, however, was not aware of this and the soldiers attacked the unsuspecting village. Many Indians, including Black Kettle, were killed. Some were taken prisoner. Once again, the army had punished peaceful Indians while hostile ones went unscathed.

In the spring of 1869, Custer cornered the last of the southern Cheyenne and then met with the chiefs in their village. The Indian leaders smoked a peace pipe with Custer and promised to stay on a reservation located in what is now western Oklahoma. In turn, Custer promised not to kill any more Cheyenne.

Although the Sioux and Cheyenne had fought each other for centuries, they had become allies by the time Custer and the Seventh Cavalry arrived on the northern Plains.

The Cheyenne were an Algonquian people originally from the northern and eastern part of the country. Their first contact with Europeans occurred in present-day Minnesota.

In the late 1600s, the Cheyenne were pushed westward by the Sioux and Ojibwa, or Chippewa. They set-tled along the river that is named for them in North Dakota, living in lodges made from dirt and sod, and farming.

About 1770, the Ojibwa attacked again. This time the Cheyenne moved onto the Plains and became semi-nomadic buffalo hunters. Eventually the Cheyenne nation split into two bands—the southern Cheyenne on the upper Arkansas River, in what is now Kansas and Colorado; and the northern Cheyenne, on the upper Platte River in what is now Nebraska and Wyoming.

At about the same time, the Ojibwa also pushed the Sioux out onto the Plains. The name *Sioux* was derived from a French translation of an Ojibwa word for "enemy." The Sioux called themselves *Lakota*—also pronounced "Dakota" and "Nakota"—which meant ally.

The Sioux were made up of seven large tribes that were divided into three groups: Dakota, Nakota, and Lakota. The Dakota lived in western Minnesota, and included the Mdewatkanton, Wahpekue, Wahpeton, and Sisseton tribes. The Nakota lived in the eastern Dakotas and included the Yankton and Yanktonais.

The Lakota or Teton tribe was larger than the other six tribes com-bined. Within the Lakota were seven subtribes: Hunkpapa, Oglala, Brule, Sans Arc (or No Bows), Two Kettles, Miniconjou, and Blackfeet.

The northern Cheyenne and the Lakota Sioux had united against the newcomers on the Plains by 1850. Each tribe and subtribe operated independently, although around 1869, some of the Lakota recognized Sitting Bull as their overall leader.

Today, there are about 12,000 Cheyenne descendants living in the United States and more than 100,000 Native Americans of Sioux heritage.

< 12 >

Then, an old Cheyenne holy man tapped his pipe against Custer's boot to knock out the burned tobacco. He warned Custer not to break his pledge. If he did, the old man said, Custer would be tracked down and killed along with all his men.

Railroads and the Panic of 1873

In 1872, the U.S. Army once again turned its attention to the northern Plains. General Ulysses S. Grant had been elected president, and Sherman had replaced him as commander of the army. Sheridan was given command of the forces in the West.

In 1873, Sheridan sent Custer into the territory that was covered by the Treaty of 1868. He and the Seventh Cavalry were supposed to protect surveyors, who had been scouting out a possible route along the Yellowstone River for the construction of the Northern Pacific Railroad. Although General David S. Stanley was the operation's commanding officer, he was often drunk, and Custer soon took charge.

Custer's main rivals in the area were Crazy Horse and the Hunkpapa chief Sitting Bull. Although he was now too old to fight, Sitting Bull remained a powerful political and spiritual figure among the Hunkpapa and other Lakota groups. Sitting Bull said of the white men and their way of life, "I have seen nothing that a white man has—houses or railways or clothing or food—that is as good as the right to...live in our own fashion."[1]

Only about 3,000 Lakota and northern Cheyenne still roamed the unceded territory. The others had moved onto the reservation. The northern Plains, which once had been too remote and inhospitable for whites, were becoming too populated for the Indians. In addition, the buffalo and other game that they depended on for food were disappearing.

When the Northern Pacific Railroad went out of business, Grant chose to open more Indian land to settlers.

In 1873, a national economic crisis bankrupted the Northern Pacific Railroad. With thousands of Americans out of work and the country in a panic, President Grant decided to open more Indian land for settlement. In the summer of 1874, Custer led ten companies of the Seventh Cavalry into the Black Hills—the sacred *Paha Sapa* of the Sioux. They were supposedly searching for a good place to build a fort to protect the Lakota Sioux from white settlers. In fact, the soldiers were there to prepare the area for white settlement.

The *Paha Sapa* was not only a place of spiritual importance for the Sioux. It was a major economic resource as well, rich in game and other foodstuffs. There were also rumors that the mountain streams glistened with gold. After those rumors were confirmed by Custer, fortune hunters flocked to the area.

Goading the Indians to Madness

The Treaty of 1868 land issue was still unsettled. The U.S. government did not want the Indians to have the land. Two chiefs, Red Cloud and Spotted Tail, were invited to Washington, D.C., to talk about setting aside the Treaty of 1868. There, the chiefs made it clear that the *Paha Sapa* was not for sale. Red Cloud was offered $6 million, but he said that it would take at least $600 million to break the treaty.

Grant, however, was in a difficult position. A presidential election year was approaching, and economic conditions jeopardized the

No American Indian was ever more controversial than Sitting Bull. His critics said that the Hunkpapa chief was a coward and a fraud. His supporters thought that he was one of the wisest, bravest, and most generous men who ever lived.

"He was regarded by the Agency Indians [on the reservation] as a great coward and a very great liar, a man with a big head and a little heart," wrote Edward S. Godfrey, a lieutenant at the Little Bighorn.[2] (Godfrey, however, apparently obtained most of his information from Gall, another Hunkpapa chief, who was one of Sitting Bull's rivals.)

"Sitting Bull is an Indian of very mediocre ability," wrote Agent James McLaughlin, "rather dull, and much the inferior of Gall and others…in intelligence. He is pompous, vain, and boastful, and considers himself a very important personage."[3]

McLaughlin, who was in charge of the Standing Rock reservation on which Sitting Bull lived during his final years, disliked the chief personally and thought him dangerous.

Others had a much higher opinion of Sitting Bull. Major James Walsh, a Northwest Mounted Police officer who knew Sitting Bull well, said, "He is the shrewdest and most intelligent Indian living, has the ambition of Napoleon and is brave to a fault.…In war he has no equal. In council he is superior to all."[4] Late in life, Sitting Bull traveled with Buffalo Bill Cody's Wild West Show. He became a close friend of the famed showman and adopted Cody's star, Annie Oakley, as his daughter.

Wooden Leg, a Cheyenne warrior who fought with the Sioux during the summer of 1876, said "I have no ears for anybody who says he was not a brave

Republican party's 16-year hold on the presidency. Many people, including Custer, believed that the Democrats would win the White House in 1876.

In November 1875, Sherman was ordered to stop keeping white trespassers out of the protected Black Hills. Next, the free-ranging Lakota under Sitting Bull were given an ultimatum—they were to go to the reservation by January 31, 1876, or be declared hostile.

man. He had a big brain, and a good one; a strong heart, and a generous one."[5]

One story perhaps best illustrates Sitting Bull's character. When the first Northern Pacific surveyors entered the Yellowstone River country, the Lakota and Cheyenne attacked them by surprise. The battle soon settled into a stalemate, with the Indians and the soldiers who were protecting the surveyors trading long range shots.

Sitting Bull finally took out his pipe and tobacco and walked out to the limit of the soldiers' rifle range. He seated himself on the ground and calmly began to smoke.

"Whoever wants to join me, come on out!" he shouted.

Two Lakota and two Cheyenne did just that. As bullets kicked up dirt around them, they sat puffing on their pipes. When he was finished smoking, Sitting Bull cleaned his pipe, slowly put it away, and strolled back to cover.

If Sitting Bull could not defeat the whites, neither would he surrender.

Chief Sitting Bull

"We are goading the Indians to madness,"[6] wrote William Curtis of the New York *World*, and that certainly seemed to be the government's intention. The government wanted war, but wanted the Sioux to start it.

The Indians had been told they must go to the reservation by the end of January 1876. The weather, which was unusually bad even for the northern Plains, made it impossible for the Indians to

< 16 >

meet this demand. Many ignored the message. Sitting Bull said that he might go the following spring.

It was obvious to Sitting Bull and to others that there would be trouble, and that it would be difficult to hold on to the *Paha Sapa*—regardless of the Treaty of 1868. Some Lakota thought it would be better to negotiate the best new deal possible for themselves. Others did not want to give up the hills, but were not ready to fight for them. Sitting Bull and Crazy Horse, however, were ready to fight.

Prelude to War

In 1876, Sheridan planned a winter campaign to take over the Black Hills, similar to the one that had succeeded in the southern Plains. Colonel John Gibbon would bring men from forts in western Montana, and General George Crook would march north from Fort Fetterman in eastern Wyoming. Meanwhile, General Alfred Terry would lead a force southwest from Fort Abraham Lincoln in the Dakota territory. Terry would be accompanied by Custer and the Seventh Cavalry. One of the coldest winters on record, however, kept the soldiers in their forts until March.

Meanwhile, Custer had been ordered to Washington, D.C., to testify in a Congressional investigation of Secretary of War William Belknap. At the hearing, Custer's outspoken criticism of the Republican party so angered Grant that the president removed Custer from the Sioux campaign. Grant eventually relented and Custer was sent back to his post. With all of the delays, however, Terry's command did not leave Fort Abraham Lincoln until late spring. In mid-June, Terry sent Custer and his men south from the Yellowstone River to find Sitting Bull. On June 25, they found him in southeast Montana on the river that the Indians called the Greasy Grass, but that the soldiers knew as the Little Bighorn.

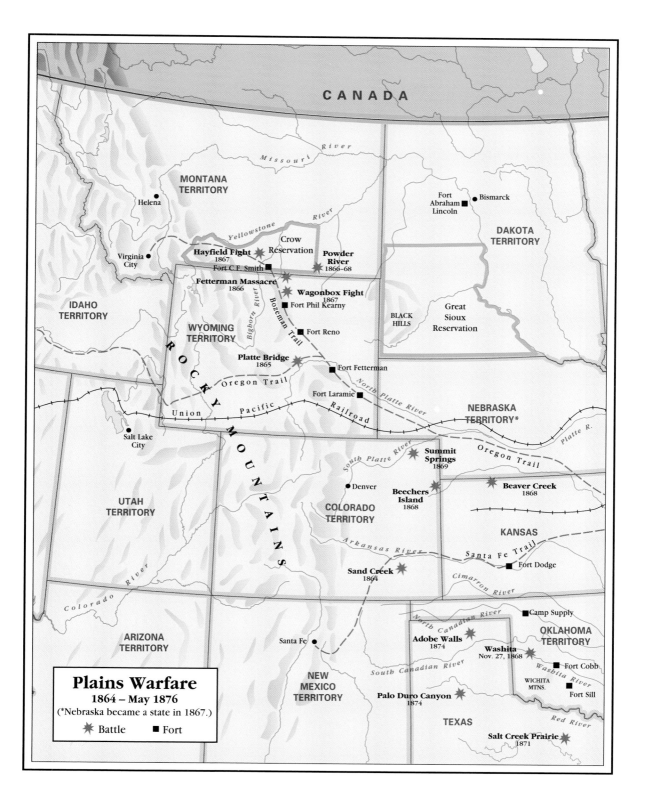

CANADA

MONTANA
TERRITORY

Helena

Virginia
City

IDAHO
TERRITORY

Missouri River

Yellowstone River

Crow
Reservation

Hayfield Fight
1867
Fort C.F. Smith

Fetterman Massacre
1866

Wagonbox Fight
1867
Fort Phil Kearny

**Powder
River**
1866–68

Fort
Abraham
Lincoln ■ Bismarck

DAKOTA
TERRITORY

Bighorn River

WYOMING
TERRITORY

Fort Reno

Bozeman Trail

BLACK
HILLS

Great
Sioux
Reservation

R O C K Y

Platte Bridge
1865

Oregon Trail

Fort Fetterman

North Platte River

Fort Laramie

M O U N T A I N S

Union   Pacific   Railroad

Salt Lake
City

UTAH
TERRITORY

South Platte River

**Summit
Springs**
1869

NEBRASKA
TERRITORY*

Oregon Trail

Platte R.

Denver

**Beechers
Island**
1868

Beaver Creek
1868

Colorado River

COLORADO
TERRITORY

Arkansas River

KANSAS

Santa Fe Trail

Fort Dodge

ARIZONA
TERRITORY

Sand Creek
1864

Cimarron River

Santa Fe

North Canadian River

Camp Supply

Adobe Walls
1874

Washita
Nov. 27, 1868

OKLAHOMA
TERRITORY

Fort Cobb

NEW
MEXICO
TERRITORY

South Canadian River

Palo Duro Canyon
1874

WICHITA
MTNS.

Washita River

Fort Sill

Plains Warfare
1864 – May 1876
(*Nebraska became a state in 1867.)

✳ Battle   ■ Fort

TEXAS

Salt Creek Prairie
1871

Red River

"SOLDIERS UPSIDE DOWN"

No one could remember ever having seen such a large gathering—not even when all seven tribes of the Lakota Sioux had once gathered in the *Paha Sapa*. During the spring of 1876, a group of 10,000 Lakota Sioux, Cheyenne, and other northern Plains Indians moved near the Yellowstone River's southern tributaries. By late June, they formed one enormous camp—a camp so large that when it moved, it left a trail a half-mile wide.

During this period in their history, Lakota camps always grew in the summer. Restless, and tired of the provisions on the reservation, families joined their friends and relatives for a few months of hunting and socializing. This year, however, things were different. The government's ultimatum that the Sioux move to the reservation, and the memory of Sand Creek, convinced the Indians that they were not safe. For the first time in eight years, more Sioux left the reservation than moved on to it.

Some historians have wondered if perhaps the Lakota and their companions realized that the battle at the Little Bighorn would be a turning point in their history. Young men who had grown up on the reservation and had never known battle headed for the Yellowstone with their fathers' hunting rifles and old war bonnets. The older men also went—to protect their land and their people.

They flocked to Sitting Bull, who was their spiritual as well as military leader. More than any Lakota before or since, Sitting Bull held the Lakota Sioux together as one nation.

"Each tribe operated its own internal government, the same as if it were entirely separated from the others," said Wooden Leg, a Cheyenne who admired Sitting Bull and fought at the Little Bighorn. "The chiefs of the different tribes met together as equals. There was only one who was considered as being above all the others. This was Sitting Bull."[1]

< 19 >

< 20 >

The Prophecies of Sitting Bull

Sitting Bull was not only a political and military leader. He was also a *Wichasha Wakan*—a spiritual leader. He experienced visions that told of the trouble ahead. In late May 1876, after three days of meditation and prayer to *Wakantanka*, the supreme being, Sitting Bull returned to his people with a strange tale.

He was sitting at the top of a butte—a flat-topped hill—when he saw dust clouds from the east rolling toward a large, white cloud that resembled a village in the hills. The clouds collided, causing a violent storm. When the storm was over, the dust clouds were gone, but the cloud shaped like an Indian village remained. According to Sitting Bull, this meant that soldiers were approaching, and that they would be defeated by the Indians.

A few weeks later, Sitting Bull held a ceremonial Sun Dance. His adopted son, Jumping Bull, cut 50 pieces of flesh from each of the chief's arms. Blood streamed from the open wounds onto the ground. Then, without food, water, or rest, Sitting Bull danced around a ceremonial pole, staring into the sun until he collapsed.

A chief named Black Moon rushed forward. Whispering, Sitting Bull described a vision of soldiers on horseback riding out of the sun toward the village. There were more soldiers than grasshoppers, said Sitting Bull, but they were upside down, and their hats were falling off. They were upside down, said Sitting Bull, because they were dead. They had no ears either, because they did not listen.

The Army Moves In

The Indians were both confident and concerned. Terry's command numbered more than 900, Gibbon's 450, and Crook's 1,300—including 250 Crow, Arikara, and Shoshoni scouts.

< 21 >

This was the first time all 12 companies of the Seventh Cavalry had been assembled in one place. Even with this large assemblage, the regiment was not at its full strength. Six of Custer's best officers had been temporarily reassigned elsewhere. On this expedition to the Black Hills his two senior officers were Captain Frederick Benteen and Major Marcus Reno, a Civil War veteran who was showing signs of losing his nerve. Neither Reno nor Benteen thought highly of Custer. "I had known General Custer for a long time," Reno said later, "and I had no confidence in him as a soldier."[2]

Reno was not alone in his view of Custer. General David S. Stanley, commanding officer of the 1873 Yellowstone expedition, wrote: "I have seen enough to convince me that he is a cold-blooded, untruthful, and un-principled man. He is univer-sally despised by all the officers of his regiment excepting his relatives and a few [others.]"[3]

Marcus Reno

Frederick Benteen

< 22 >

Perhaps because of such unfavorable opinions, Custer kept his family near him. His wife Elizabeth accompanied him whenever possible. On this particular expedition, Custer had also brought along his brothers Tom and Boston, his nephew Autie Reed, and his brother-in-law James Calhoun.

The winter campaign planned by Sheridan had misfired. The Seventh Cavalry and the other men under Terry's command did not leave Fort Abraham Lincoln until May 17. Now it was spring, and although the weather was better, most of the officers believed that their job would be more difficult. Everyone knew that when the winter camps broke up, the Indians would become scattered throughout the territories. Custer had said that the hardest part about fighting Indians was finding them.

Marching into the Unknown

Terry did not know the whereabouts of the Indians he was chasing. His best guess was that they were positioned along the Little Missouri River, putting them 150 miles east of their actual location. Nor did Terry have any idea of the size of the Indian forces. In fact, none of the officers knew or cared, Custer least of all, whether there were 500 or 5,000 Indians—they did not think that overpowering the Indians would be difficult. Because of this outlook, the officers in the campaign greatly underestimated the strength of the Sioux and Cheyenne.

There were enough clues, however, for Terry, Custer, and the others to begin suspecting that something was going on. Crook, who seemed to understand Indians better than any other officer, was especially cautious. Gibbon's Crow scouts, commanded by Lieutenant James Bradley, tried to warn the soldiers of the danger ahead, but they were ignored.

Indian scouts watched Custer advance and sent warnings ahead.

The army barreled forward. On June 7, Terry and Gibbon met on the Yellowstone River. Communications were so poor, however, that Terry had only the faintest idea where Crook and his men were. The same applied to Crook's knowledge of Terry's whereabouts. And yet the officers remained confident.

The Indians, on the other hand, had a good idea of the soldiers' location. They had been told about Crook by relatives and friends coming from the reservation. They also brought news that Custer, who they called Long Hair, was on his way.

< 24 >

A few days after Sitting Bull's Sun Dance vision, several Cheyenne returned to camp with the news that the Rosebud Creek Valley was black with soldiers. This swarm was Crook's army.

Battle of the Rosebud

Unlike the other officers, Crook studied Indians. He insisted on recruiting them not only as scouts against their traditional enemies, but also to fight their own tribesmen. Crook was known for being completely and brutally honest. "Surrender and I will be your best friend," he told them. "Resist and I will track you down and kill you to the last man."[4]

When the Cheyenne scouts spotted Crook, the camp elders decided to try to avoid a fight. A large number of young Cheyenne were eager to prove themselves, however, and sneaked off to attack the army. Once this was discovered, Crazy Horse and other war chiefs organized about 1,000 warriors to attack Crook's party.

Rosebud Creek, a tributary of the Yellowstone River, flows to the east of the Bighorn and Little Bighorn Rivers. Moving his men with a discipline rare among Plains warriors, Crazy Horse led an overnight march that caught Crook's command by surprise on the morning of June 17. It was a furious, day-long fight largely between Crook's Shoshoni and Crow scouts and the warriors under Crazy Horse and Two Moons. The countryside was rough, and neither side could get the advantage of the other. "Sometimes we chased them," said Wooden Leg, "sometimes they chased us."[5] At nightfall, the Lakota and Cheyenne withdrew. Crook declared victory and retreated with his men to the south.

The Indians, however, had actually won an important victory. They had turned Crook back and depleted his supplies, and so put his party out of action for months. (One problem with large forces

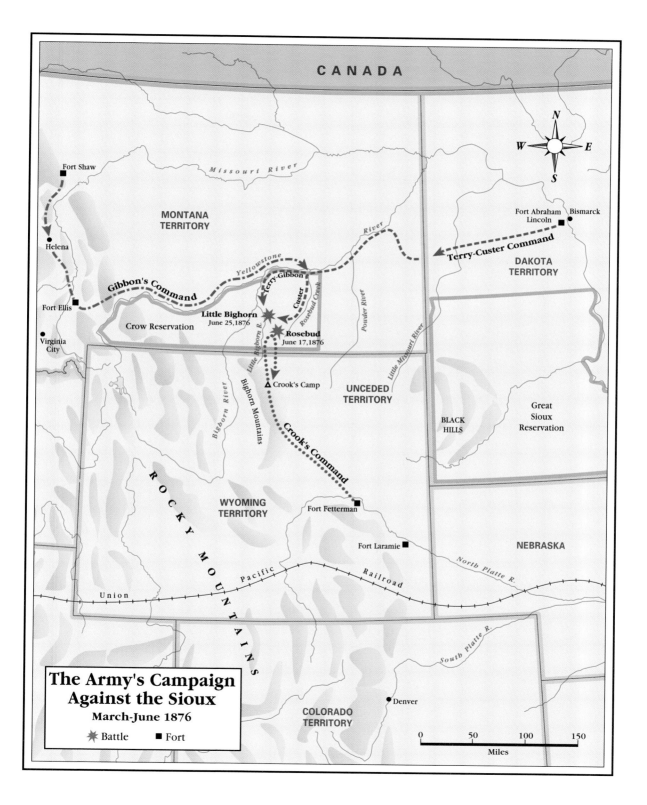

CANADA

Missouri River

MONTANA
TERRITORY

Fort Shaw

Helena

Fort Ellis

Virginia
City

Fort Abraham
Lincoln · Bismarck

DAKOTA
TERRITORY

Terry-Custer Command

River

Yellowstone

Gibbon's Command

Terry-Gibbon

Custer

Little Bighorn
June 25,1876

Crow Reservation

Rosebud
June 17,1876

Rosebud Creek

Powder River

△ Crook's Camp

Little Missouri River

Little Bighorn R.

Bighorn River

Bighorn Mountains

UNCEDED
TERRITORY

BLACK
HILLS

Great
Sioux
Reservation

Crook's Command

R O C K Y   M O U N T A I N S

WYOMING
TERRITORY

Fort Fetterman

Fort Laramie

NEBRASKA

North Platte R.

Union   Pacific   Railroad

South Platte R.

Denver

COLORADO
TERRITORY

The Army's Campaign
Against the Sioux
March-June 1876

✶ Battle   ■ Fort

0   50   100   150
Miles

< 26 >

on the frontier was that they used up supplies quickly. Unlike the Indians, the army was not good at "living off the land.") When Custer and the Seventh Cavalry came along a week later, the Indians were ready for them.

A Big Fight

While Crook and Crazy Horse were fighting on the upper Rosebud, Reno and six troops of the Seventh Cavalry were scouting south of the Yellowstone. They came across the trail of Sitting Bull's big camp. It was heading west, over the ridge that separated the Rosebud and Little Bighorn valleys.

Equipped with this information, Terry, Custer, Gibbon, and Gibbon's second in command, Major James Brisbin—a colorful character known as "Grasshopper Jim"—met a few days later, aboard the steamboat *Far West*, anchored in the Yellowstone.

Brisbin later insisted that Custer and Terry were informed at this meeting that Bradley's Crow scouts estimated the opposing forces at 3,000 men. Bloody Knife, Custer's favorite Arikara scout, was also concerned about the large Indian gathering. Another scout, named Mitch Bouyer, told Lieutenant Edward S. Godfrey, "I can tell you we are going to have a...big fight."[6]

The senior officers were not impressed by this information. They were more worried that the Indians would run away to the Bighorn Mountains in the south. First and foremost, said Gibbon, the officers wanted "to prevent the escape of the Indians, which was the idea pervading the minds of us all."[7]

To prevent them from escaping to the south and into the mountains, the officers devised a plan to get behind the Indians. The entire Seventh Cavalry, approximately 600 men, would head down the Rosebud with Custer and then turn west. With a little

< 27 >

luck, the officers thought, Custer might run into Crook's group. They did not know that Crook was back in Wyoming, fishing for trout and waiting for his men to recover from the battle at Rosebud Creek on June 17.

While Custer circled to the south, Terry and Gibbon were to head down the Bighorn River to the mouth of the Little Bighorn. If all went well, they would meet up with Custer on June 26. The plan was to trap the Indians between Custer's men and those of Terry and Gibbon.

The Seventh Cavalry was expected to do most of the fighting. Brisbin's suggestion that Custer take four companies from Gibbon's Second Cavalry was rejected—perhaps because Terry did not think it was practical. Custer was also offered Gatling guns—cumbersome forerunners of the machine gun—which he refused. He said that they would only slow him down.

Custer had a reputation for acting recklessly and without regard for the odds or for his own safety. Yet things always seemed to work out for him. "Custer's Luck" was well known in the army, and Custer himself seemed to believe that he could not be beaten.

Custer and his men marched up Rosebud Creek and west toward the Little Bighorn. They covered 72 miles in 3 days—a long journey, but not an unusual distance for the cavalry. After stumbling through the dark on the night of June 24, they arrived near the top of the ridge that separated the Rosebud and Little Bighorn valleys. With the Sioux and Cheyenne barely 15 miles away, Custer allowed the men to rest while the enemy was scouted and battle plans were drawn.

At the first light of dawn, however, Custer's Crow scouts began chanting death songs. One scout, Hairy Moccasin, had spotted the huge gathering of Sioux and Cheyenne. While this confirmed the Crow and Arikara scouts' worst fears, it spurred Custer to swifter action.

According to biographer Frederic Van de Water, George Armstrong Custer "was one of the healthiest, most vital men who ever lived, almost immune to hunger and thirst, heat and cold, sleepiness and fatigue."[8]

He was certainly a man of action. Through a lively childhood and four years at the U.S. Military Academy at West Point, Custer often seemed on the edge of disaster. But he always managed to escape from trouble.

"The great difficulty is that he is too clever for his own good," said a friend. "He is always connected with all the mischief that is going on, and never studies any more than he can possibly help."[9]

At West Point, Custer was called Curly because of his tangle of golden hair. It was a name he shared with his rival, Crazy Horse. Indifferent to discipline and tradition, Custer collected so many demerits (bad behavior points) that he ranked last in the academy's Class of 1861.

Yet within a year, Custer was an aide to the Union army's commanding officer, Major General George McClellan. Within two years, Custer became a general himself, just in time to become a hero of the battle of Gettysburg in the Civil War.

George Custer

Riding to the lookout point of Hairy Moccasin and the other scouts, Custer decided to begin the attack immediately. The scout Bouyer warned Custer that this was the largest gathering of Indians he had seen in more than 30 years. The Arikara muttered *Otoe Sioux! Otoe Sioux!*, which means "too many Sioux, too many Sioux."

Custer was always a dramatic figure in action. He often dashed around the battlefield waving his saber and his pistols. He made an inviting target, but always escaped serious harm.

"The rebs say they dasent [dare not] shoot a cannon for if they do general Custer is shure to go for it and take it away from them," said one of Custer's men.[10] Most of the soldiers loved him, as did his superiors. His rivals, however, thought that Custer was a fool.

"The truth about Custer is that he was a pet soldier who had risen not above his merit but higher than men of equal merit," said one officer when news of the Little Bighorn reached the East. "He fought with Phil Sheridan and through the patronage of Sheridan he rose, but while Sheridan liked his valor and his dash, he never trusted his judgment. We all think...he sacrificed the Seventh Cavalry to ambition and wounded vanity."[11]

Custer fought under Sheridan during the final months of the Civil War. The older officer was so impressed by Custer's aggressiveness that after the war, when Sheridan was sent to subdue the Plains Indians, he took Custer along.

Custer brought his fiery spirit to the West. He wrote articles for *Galaxy* magazine about Indian fighting and hunting, which added to the Custer legend. In 1874, he published the articles as a book, *My Life on the Plains*. This inflated his reputation even more.

"My every thought was ambitious," Custer once wrote of himself, "not to be wealthy, not to be learned, but to be great. I desired to link my name with acts and men, and in such manner as to be a mark of honor, not only to the present but to future generations."[12]

But Custer had already made up his mind. He believed that the Indians had spotted them and that there was no time left.

Right before the soldiers were to march, Godfrey went to Custer's tent. He found him with Bloody Knife and several other scouts, as well as an interpreter. Recalled Godfrey:

Custer sits surrounded by loyal Arikara scouts, including Bloody Knife (kneeling on Custer's right).

> *The scouts were doing the talking, and seemed nervous and disturbed. Finally Bloody Knife made a remark...and [Custer] asked in his usual quick, brusque manner, `What's that he says!' The interpreter replied: `He says we'll find enough Sioux to keep us fighting two or three days.' The General smiled and remarked, `I guess we'll get through with them in one day.'[13]*

Custer Divides His Forces

About noon on June 25, the Seventh Cavalry crossed the divide between the two valleys. The regiment was split into four battalions (groupings of companies). Companies A, G, and M, totaling 140 officers and men, were under the command of Reno. Companies D, H, and K, totaling about 125 men, were under Benteen's command. Custer

< 31 >

maintained command of Companies C, I, L, E, and F. This battalion was later split into two wings. The first wing consisted of Companies E and F, led by Captain George W. Yates. The second wing, Companies C, I, and L, were led by Captain Myles Keogh. A fourth batallion, Company B, was detached to escort the packtrain—mules and horses carrying supplies, such as food and ammunition.

Custer told Benteen to swing around to the south and make sure there were no hostile forces further upstream. This was to protect the main body of soldiers from being attacked from the rear when they entered the Little Bighorn valley.

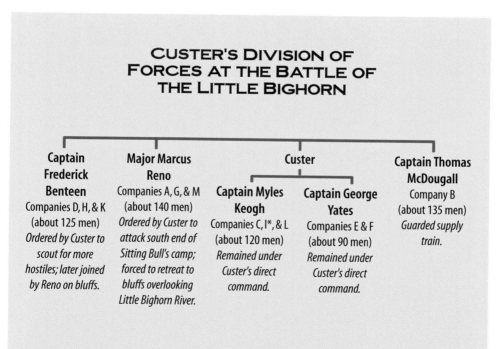

CUSTER'S DIVISION OF FORCES AT THE BATTLE OF THE LITTLE BIGHORN

Captain Frederick Benteen	Major Marcus Reno	Custer		Captain Thomas McDougall
Companies D, H, & K (about 125 men) Ordered by Custer to scout for more hostiles; later joined by Reno on bluffs.	Companies A, G, & M (about 140 men) Ordered by Custer to attack south end of Sitting Bull's camp; forced to retreat to bluffs overlooking Little Bighorn River.	Captain Myles Keogh Companies C, I*, & L (about 120 men) Remained under Custer's direct command.	Captain George Yates Companies E & F (about 90 men) Remained under Custer's direct command.	Company B (about 135 men) Guarded supply train.

*There was no Company J.

< 32 >

Custer and his men approached the Little Bighorn River down a stream that today is called Reno Creek. Along the way, he became increasingly convinced that the Indians had seen his men and now were trying to escape. Warriors were seen riding toward the village they had created. A dust cloud rose from behind a ridge, which seemed to indicate that the big camp was on the move. Custer pushed his men harder.

He ordered Reno to cross the Little Bighorn, and to charge the southern end of the village. "You will be supported by the whole outfit," Custer said.[14] However, instead of backing Reno, Custer and his men rode north.

The Indians Stand Firm

Although the Sioux and Cheyenne camp was extremely large, it moved in an orderly fashion. The Cheyenne were always in the lead and Sitting Bull's Hunkpapa Lakota brought up the rear. The other Lakota bands and a few bands of Arapaho and Santee Sioux traveled in their own groups between the Cheyenne and Lakota.

Whenever the camp stopped moving, it always had the same formation—circles of tipis with the Cheyenne at one end and the Hunkpapa at the other.

Reno attacked the camp at the Hunkpapa end and caught the Indians by surprise. The Hunkpapa knew soldiers might come, but expected Crook's men from the south. Women and children scrambled for safety, and the men for their guns and horses, as Reno's battalion charged across the Little Bighorn. One Lakota woman, She Who Walks With Her Shawl, was 23 years old that morning:

When I got to my tent, mother told me that . . . my brother had been killed. . . . I heard Hawkman shout, 'Ho-ka-he! Ho-ka-he!' . . . . The

< 33 >

soldiers began firing into our camp. . . . I saw my father preparing to go to battle. . . .

My heart was bad. Revenge! Revenge! . . . I ran to a nearby thicket and got my black horse. I painted my face crimson and unbraided my black hair. . . . I was a woman, but I was not afraid.[15]

The Lakota war cry, *Ho-ka-he! Ho-ka-he!*, and the shrill, piercing scream of eagle bone whistles filled the air.

Crazy Horse, in the Oglala circle, shouted: "It is a good day to fight! It is a good day to die! Strong hearts, brave hearts to the front! Weak hearts and cowards to the rear!"[16]

Reno Retreats

The Indians who defended the southern end of the village said later that they believed Reno's soldiers must have been either drunk or crazy. After the initial attack, the soldiers made a hasty retreat. They first hid in some trees along the river. They then ran across open ground and swam back across the river, where they tried to scramble up the bluffs. Forty men, about one fourth of Reno's battalion, were killed in the attempt.

Unlike Custer, Reno was concerned about the size of the Indian camp facing him—especially after Custer, who had promised to support Reno with "the whole outfit," had disappeared over a ridge. Historians today believe that the strange actions of the soldiers under Reno's command that day were the result of a panic that spread throughout the battalion.

For the rest of his life, Reno was blamed for what happened at the Little Bighorn. Most of his men, however, saw it differently. "(I)f we had gone five hundred yards farther we would have been

This drawing depicting Reno's retreat was done by a Northern Cheyenne Indian named White Bird.

butchered," said Lieutenant Camilius De Rudio, and his fellow officers agreed.[17]

During the battle, the Lakota Sioux fell on Reno's men with clubs, hatchets, tomahawks, and guns. Two soldiers lost control of their horses and rode right into the middle of the Hunkpapa circle. They were not greeted warmly.

She Who Walks With Her Shawl recalled:

The Greasy Grass [Little Bighorn River] was very deep. [The soldiers'] horses had to swim to get across. Some of the warriors rode into the water and tomahawked the soldiers. In the charge the Indians rode among the troopers and with tomahawks unhorsed several of them....The Indians chased the soldiers across the river and up over a bluff.[18]

< 35 >

Custer's Attack

As Reno's men were clambering up the northern embankment of the Little Bighorn, more soldiers were attacking several miles downstream, near the north end of the big camp.

It has never been determined why Custer pulled his five companies away from Reno's battalion. Some think that he had no firm plan. Others believe Custer assumed that Reno would continue his attack and that Benteen would soon return. Custer may also have thought the Indians were attempting to surround him. Shortly after his battalions left Reno, 60 to 75 mounted warriors were seen galloping along the ridge above the river. Moments later, Custer's five companies set off at a gallop in parallel columns of two.

They rode north up the gently sloping bank. Near the crest, Custer and his orderly Giovanni Martini—an Italian immigrant called John Martin by the soldiers—as well as several Crow scouts went on ahead. The entire Indian camp was laid out before them. To the south, Reno's men were engaged in a desperate fight against Indians whom Custer had assumed were running away.

Upon seeing the camp, Martini said that Custer waved his hat in the air and shouted, "Hurrah boys we've got them!"[19]

If this account is accurate—and many historians have their doubts—Custer was either trying to encourage his men or he had completely misunderstood the situation. Since his subsequent actions seem to indicate that he *did* understand, Custer may have been trying to motivate his men to fight.

Custer sent Sergeant Daniel Kanipe to bring up the packtrain. Every man and every bullet would be needed. Custer then took the soldiers, riding single file, into a long ravine that led down to the Little Bighorn. Custer probably thought that he would be able to cross the river there.

< 36 >

Custer turned to Martini and ordered him to find Benteen and urge him to hurry. Martini had not been in the United States long, though, and did not understand English well. Custer's aide, W.W. Cooke, realized this and scribbled the order on a piece of paper. It read:

Benteen. Come On. Be Quick. Bring Packs.
W.W. Cooke
P.S. bring packs.[20]

The Indians Counterattack

As Martini set out to find Benteen, he looked back to see Custer and his men disappearing into the ravine.

Custer soon divided his command again. Yates's two companies were sent down the ravine into a deep, dry creekbed called Medicine Tail Coulee. Keogh's three companies were positioned on the ridge between Medicine Tail and another dry creekbed, called Deep Coulee.

This decision may have resulted from the information brought by Custer's youngest brother, Boston. Hurrying forward from the packtrain, Boston Custer had learned that Benteen had finished his information-gathering mission. He probably told his brother to expect Benteen to arrive soon.

Custer may have intended for Yates to hold the east side of the Little Bighorn, with support from Keogh's men, until Benteen arrived. Yates may even have tried to cross the river and attack the Cheyenne end of the big village. Either way, Custer was soon overwhelmed.

Despite the urgency of the message delivered to Benteen by Martini, Benteen later claimed that Martini had given him the

A soldier is unhorsed by an Indian warrior during the battle of Little Bighorn.

impression that Custer was in control of the situation. Benteen said that his horses were tired and that Reno's besieged troops appeared to need him more. In any event, he was slow to respond to Custer's appeal. By the time Benteen realized the seriousness of Custer's position, it was too late. The Sioux and Cheyenne had cut Custer's troops off from help.

Only a few Indians confronted Yates's men as they emerged from Medicine Tail Coulee onto the Little Bighorn. Their numbers increased quickly, however, to as many as 1,500 Indians in just a few minutes.

< 38 >

George W. Yates

Myles Keogh

The Indians were well armed. Many carried Colt revolvers, and others had repeating Winchester and Henry rifles. Although these guns were not as accurate as the soldiers' single-shot Springfields, they were deadlier at close range because they could be fired many times without reloading. Sitting Bull, who was observing the battle from a nearby bluff, said later, "Our men rained lead across the river and drove the white braves back."[21]

Already outnumbered, Custer was nearly surrounded. Warriors under Crazy Horse and the Cheyenne Chief Two Moons were circling north behind the hills that the soldiers were now attempting to reach. Yates's men tried to make an orderly retreat, but they were being jerked around by their frightened horses. This made it difficult for them to shoot accurately. "The horses were so frightened that they pulled the men all around, and a great many of their shots went up in the air and did us no harm," a warrior named Low Dog said later.[22]

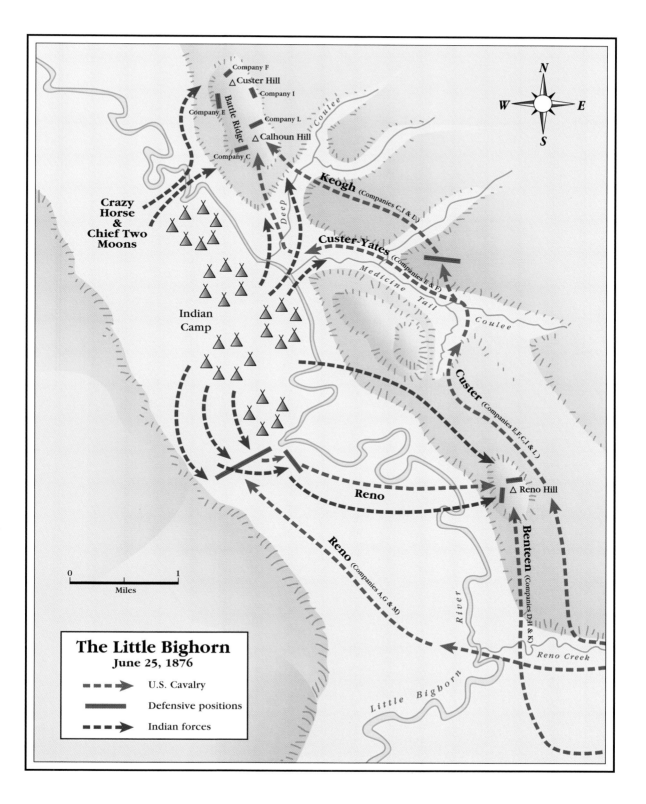

Company F
△ Custer Hill
Company I
Company L
Battle Ridge
Company E
△ Calhoun Hill
Company C

Keogh (Companies C,I & L)

Crazy Horse & Chief Two Moons

Custer-Yates (Companies E & F)

Deep

Coulee

Medicine Tail

Indian Camp

Coulee

Custer (Companies E,F,C,I & L)

Reno

△ Reno Hill

Reno (Companies A,G & M)

Benteen (Companies D,H & K)

River

Reno Creek

Little Bighorn

0   1
Miles

The Little Bighorn
June 25, 1876

- - → U.S. Cavalry

——— Defensive positions

- - → Indian forces

< 40 >

As Keogh's group moved north to higher ground, the men dismounted in order to fire back at the Indians. The men assigned to hold the horses were shot, causing the animals to stampede and carry away all the spare ammunition. The surviving soldiers now had only their pistols.

The Last Stand

What remained of Yates's and Keogh's companies joined up on what is now called Calhoun Hill. Named for Custer's brother-in-law, the commanding officer of Company L, the hill provided a sweeping view of the valley below and the distant mountains. It also provided the only possible escape route—a series of hills and ravines to the east and the north.

At this point, Custer sent a company of men to stop some Indians trying to get around the soldiers on the west. After initial success, the soldiers were thrown back by a group of Cheyenne.

Indians were streaming up the Deep Coulee. Keogh tried to hold them off while Yates—and probably Custer—fought their way to another hill along what is now known as Battle Ridge. Here they made what was to be their last stand.

Arriving on the crest of the hill just ahead of Custer, Crazy Horse paused briefly, perhaps to take in the scene below. He was a striking figure among his painted, war-bonneted companions, wearing his customary single feather, a charm behind one ear and another under his arm. Custer was probably only a few yards away, and almost certainly he saw Crazy Horse.

When Crazy Horse appeared, the soldiers that were still fighting knew their situation was hopeless. He had blocked the last way out. Swooping down, Crazy Horse and his men delivered their final blows to the doomed soldiers.

Custer's men make their last stand against Crazy Horse and his warriors.

Custer and about 40 of his men, including his brothers, Autie Reed, Yates, and Cooke, shot their horses for cover. All of these men, however, were killed on what is now known as Custer Hill. Keogh fell nearby. About 30 soldiers tried to break free and headed down

< 42 >

a ravine. They were surrounded by the Indian warriors and killed. Calhoun never made it off the hill that was later named for him.

In the final moments of the battle, Crazy Horse was everywhere, fighting and urging his men amidst the swirling dust and thick gunsmoke. The dust clouds were so dense that people in the village across the river could not see past them. They were so thick that the warriors in them were surprised to find that all the soldiers were dead—or were too wounded to fight. Those still alive were finished off with clubs, tomahawks, and guns.

Estimates of Indian casualties vary widely. When the fighting ended, women from the Indian camp went to remove their dead and wounded relatives from the battlefield and to take revenge on the bodies of the soldiers. Two of the women were southern Cheyenne who had survived the battle of the Washita. They came across Custer's body, which was about to be cut into pieces by some Sioux men.

The women remembered Monahsetah, Custer's so-called "Indian wife" who had been a prisoner after the Sand Creek battle. She became Custer's guide and interpreter, and still waited for him on the Cheyenne reservation in Oklahoma. Monahsetah had a son whom the Indians believed was Custer's. The women asked the Sioux warriors to leave Custer's body alone. He was, they said, a relative.

But they were angry with him. The women shoved the sharp point of a sewing awl into both of his ears. He had not listened when the old chief had warned Custer not to attack the Cheyenne again. The awl, explained the women, would improve Custer's hearing.

The Price of Victory

The next afternoon Sitting Bull decided that it was time to leave. The Indians couldn't overrun the soldiers on the bluffs, and Terry and Gibbon were approaching from the north. The younger men

< 43 >

still wanted to fight, but the elders were against it. They knew their great victory would carry a terrible price.

The U.S. Army reacted swiftly, if not effectively. Terry and Crook spent most of the summer searching the northern Plains for Indians, but did not find many. Custer's worst fear had been realized. The big camp had split up and its inhabitants had scattered.

East of the Little Bighorn in the Dakota territory, at Slim Buttes, a detachment of soldiers looking for food stumbled upon a small Indian village. The Indians there denied having been at the Little Bighorn, but soldiers found clothing and other souvenirs of the battle. Enraged, the soldiers burned everything, leaving the Lakota without food or shelter as the winter approached.

The U.S. government then went after the Indians living on the reservation. All food and other supplies were withheld from the Indians until the sacred Black Hills—the *Paha Sapa*—were signed over to the government.

In October, General Nelson Miles arrived. A clever and ambitious man, Miles divided his command into small, mobile units. Through freezing rain and waist-deep snow, Miles and his men pursued the Indians. Although they rarely fought pitched battles, the soldiers kept their adversaries always on the move. When they did fight the Indians—at Cedar Creek, at Ash Creek, and in the Wolf Mountains—the soldiers won.

Further south, in Wyoming, Crook's men attacked the Cheyenne village of Dull Knife. Here, too, the toll was measured not so much in the number of Indians killed or wounded, but in the amount of dried meat destroyed and the number of lodges and buffalo robes burned. The Indians who survived the attack were left to wander without food or shelter in the cold November snow.

Becoming discouraged, the Sioux and Cheyenne began heading for the reservation. In May, Sitting Bull left the Plains and went to

As a boy, Crazy Horse was called Curly. It was an unusual name for an Oglala Lakota Sioux.

His light wavy hair, fair skin, wiry build, and sharp features were distinctive among the Oglala. More than once he heard it suggested that his parents were white, and that he was the adopted son of the holy man also called Crazy Horse. That was not true.

If Crazy Horse's appearance caused comment, his behavior was an even greater source of gossip. Crazy Horse was a loner. He took no part in the *akicity*—warrior societies—and avoided the usual social activities of other Oglala men. He didn't tell jokes, sing, or brag. He married late and only once. His own people referred to Crazy Horse as The Strange One, but that did not prevent them from holding him in the highest esteem.

"Crazy Horse always led his men himself when they went into battle, and he kept well in front of them," said a warrior named He Dog. "He headed many charges."[23]

Among the Plains Indians, the chief objective of war was not to kill the enemy, but to prove one's own courage by *counting coup*—touching an opponent with a special stick—and stealing ponies. Firing rifles at each other from behind trees and boulders the way white men did seemed pointless. White man's war, the Plains Indians said, was just shooting.

But "just shooting" was very deadly. In the Powder River War and later in the Yellowstone country, Crazy Horse learned the Indians had to fight more like soldiers. "All the times I was in fights with Crazy Horse, in critical moments of the fight Crazy Horse would always jump off his horse to fire," said He Dog. "He is the only Indian I ever knew who did that often. He wanted to be sure that he hit what he aimed at.… He didn't like to start a battle unless he had it all planned out in his head and knew he was going to win."[24]

The Indian allies were not as organized or as disciplined as most army units, but they were much more organized and disciplined than Indians on the northern Plains had ever been before.

After the Little Bighorn, Crazy Horse led his people into the mountains, vowing that he would never give up. Through a brutal winter he fought

Crazy Horse

the soldiers of Crook and Miles. Finally, for the good of his people, he surrendered. The defeated Indians rode into Camp Robinson, Nebraska, in a long, dignified procession, with Crazy Horse in the lead.

"This is a triumphal march," exclaimed an officer, "not a surrender."[25]

The dead are loaded onto carts after the battle of Wounded Knee.

Canada. Crazy Horse remained until spring, and then rode ceremoniously into Crook's headquarters at Camp Robinson, Nebraska. Six months later Crazy Horse was dead—bayoneted by a soldier when the army tried to put him in prison.

In 1881, Sitting Bull returned to the United States from Canada. He toured the East with Buffalo Bill's Wild West Show and would have gone to Europe if the government had allowed it. In December 1890, the reservation's Indian police went to Sitting Bull's home to arrest him on false charges. A riot resulted and Sitting Bull was shot and killed.

A few days later, members of the Seventh Cavalry slaughtered a scared, starving band of Lakota at Wounded Knee, South Dakota. The 400-year fight for America was over. The fight at Little Bighorn, on the windswept plains of southeastern Montana, had been more than a battle. Sitting Bull had seen it as two great storms colliding—and so it had been. The resulting violence was so sudden and powerful that it caught both the Indians and the white men by surprise. When the storm passed, the Indians realized that their long war was finally and irreversibly lost.

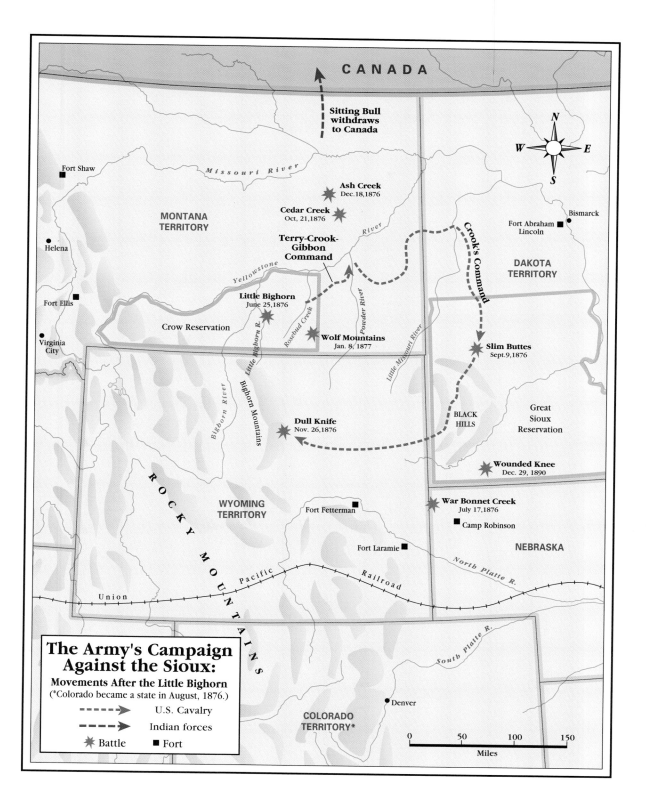

CANADA

Sitting Bull
withdraws
to Canada

Fort Shaw

Missouri River

Ash Creek
Dec.18, 1876

Cedar Creek
Oct, 21, 1876

MONTANA
TERRITORY

River

Crook's Command

Fort Abraham
Lincoln

Bismarck

Helena

**Terry-Crook-
Gibbon
Command**

Yellowstone

DAKOTA
TERRITORY

Fort Ellis

Little Bighorn
June 25, 1876

Crow Reservation

Little Bighorn R.

Rosebud Creek

Powder River

Wolf Mountains
Jan. 8, 1877

Little Missouri River

Virginia
City

Bighorn River

Bighorn Mountains

Dull Knife
Nov. 26, 1876

BLACK
HILLS

Slim Buttes
Sept.9, 1876

Great
Sioux
Reservation

Wounded Knee
Dec. 29, 1890

R O C K Y

WYOMING
TERRITORY

Fort Fetterman

War Bonnet Creek
July 17, 1876

Camp Robinson

NEBRASKA

M

Fort Laramie

O

North Platte R.

U

N

Pacific

Railroad

T

Union

A

I

South Platte R.

N

S

Denver

The Army's Campaign
Against the Sioux:
Movements After the Little Bighorn
(*Colorado became a state in August, 1876.)

- - - →   U.S. Cavalry

— — →   Indian forces

✳ Battle   ■ Fort

COLORADO
TERRITORY*

N
W   E
S

| 0 | 50 | 100 | 150 |

Miles

HISTORY REMEMBERED

Battle sites have long been remembered, both for their importance to history and as a reminder of the sacrifices made by those who fought. The dust of battle had barely settled when people began calling for a Little Bighorn memorial.

In 1879, a national cemetery was created to protect the graves of the soldiers buried along the Little Bighorn. Later, it was named the National Cemetery of Custer's Battlefield Reservation. In 1926, the Reno-Benteen Battlefield was created, and in 1946, the two were renamed the Custer Battlefield National Monument.

As these names suggest, the cemetery and the surrounding grounds honored only the U.S. soldiers who died at the Little Bighorn. The Indians who fought there were almost completely ignored.

This angered many American Indians. A number of white people agreed that this was unfair. The Indians at the Little Bighorn, after all, had only been doing what they had been given every right to do under the Treaty of 1868. They were in their own territory, hunting buffalo and doing their best to stay out of the white men's way. Despite these facts, they had been attacked.

The U.S. government and the National Park Service have taken steps to recognize the Indians. In 1991, President George Bush changed the name of Custer Battlefield National Monument to Little Bighorn Battlefield National Monument. A site was designated for a memorial to Indians who fought in the battle.

< 49 >

The Little Bighorn battlefield is almost as remote today as it was at the time of the battle.

"A Message for the Living"

The Park Service is sponsoring a design contest for this memorial based on themes suggested by two Lakota elders who are now deceased, Austin Two Moons and Enos Poor Bear. Some have suggested the soldiers, and particularly Custer, be portrayed more unflatteringly than in the past—and certainly not as heroes.

Two Moons and Poor Bear, however, disagreed and felt that both sides should be represented fairly. "If this memorial is to serve its total purpose," said Poor Bear, "it must contain a message for the living. We strongly suggest to you that power through unity would serve us well."[1]

Recent Archaeological Findings

Another compelling reason to preserve battle sites is that they can continue to provide clues about the fight for decades to come. Although objects from skeletons to uniform buttons have been recovered in the vicinity since the late 1870s, little archaeological work was done on the Little Bighorn battlefield until 1984.

< 51 >

In 1983, a grass fire made an extensive search of the site possible. Using metal detectors and modern archaeological methods, hundreds of artifacts were unearthed from the bare ground. Among these were bullets and shell casings, which indicated that at least 42 different types of firearms were used in the battle of the Little Bighorn.

These artifacts supplied new information on a variety of questions, including what sort of weapons the Indians used during the battle, how the army's weapons performed, and exactly how many soldiers actually died with Custer.

Researchers also tried to clear up a mystery regarding the marble markers placed on the battlefield in 1890. The markers replaced wooden ones that had been used to mark the spots where bodies were found after the battle in 1876. Although Custer was thought to have only about 210 men with him, there are 252 markers. The

In 1890, these marble markers replaced wooden markers that indicated where soldiers were killed during the battle.

< 52 >

researchers concluded that this was the result of a misunderstanding and that the extra markers were actually meant for men who were killed at the Reno-Benteen battle site.

Somewhat surprisingly, few of the men who died at the Little Bighorn are buried in the actual cemetery. The Lakota and Cheyenne took their casualties away. The soldiers killed were hastily buried where they fell. In 1881, most were reburied in a mass grave on Custer Hill. Thus, the cemetery contains mostly the remains of soldiers killed in other battles or those who died natural deaths.

Among those whose remains did not stay on the battlefield was Custer. His remains were reburied on the grounds of the U.S. Military Academy in 1877. The remains of Major Reno, who died in Washington, D.C., were brought to the Custer National cemetery in 1967.

Little Bighorn Battlefield National Monument

The battlefield is nearly as remote by today's standards as it was in 1876. It is in the middle of the Crow Reservation. In addition to the preserved cemetery, the 4.5-mile-long Battlefield Road follows the progress of the battle, from Reno's position on the bluffs overlooking the Little Bighorn River, to Battle Ridge.

Location and Address Little Bighorn Battlefield National Monument, P.O. Box 190, Crow Agency, MT 59022. Telephone: (406) 638-2621.

Operating Hours 8 A.M.–8 P.M., Memorial Day through Labor Day; until 6 P.M. in the spring and fall; and until 4:30 P.M. in the winter.

Entrance Fees $6.00 per private vehicle; $3.00 per pedestrian.

Exhibits and Events The battle is constantly recreated in the minds of historians and others fascinated by the events of that day. A cast of 300 reenacts the battle every year during Little Bighorn Days in late June. The script for the reenactment relies heavily on

Custer's last stand at Little Bighorn is reenacted every June at Little Bighorn Battlefield National Monument.

< 54 >

accounts of Crow tribal history. Participants include descendants of those on both sides of the original battle. (Ironically, the battlefield lies within the reservation of the Crow Indians, some of whom served as guides for the U.S. Army at Little Bighorn. Each year in August, the Crow Fair takes place. It is the largest gathering of Native Americans in the country. A rodeo, powwow, and riding exhibitions are held.) The Visitor Center and museum includes displays of artifacts and battle scenes. It is located near the Seventh Cavalry Monument and the proposed site for the Indian memorial. Rangers lead tours of the battle site.

Related Points of Interest

Crazy Horse Memorial

Deep within the sacred *Paha Sapa*—the Black Hills—is the massive Crazy Horse Memorial. Korczak Ziolkowski, an assistant who worked on the nearby Mount Rushmore project, began blasting the figure of Crazy Horse out of a mountain five miles north of Custer, South Dakota, in 1948, seven years after receiving a letter from Lakota

The model in the foreground shows what the Crazy Horse Memorial will look like when it is completed.

< 55 >

Chief Henry Standing Bear. The Sioux, said Standing Bear, wanted the white man to know "the red man has great heroes, too."

Ziolkowski labored mostly alone until his death in 1982. Since then, his wife Ruth and seven of their ten children have continued his work. They expect to finish in the year 2000. When completed, the 563-foot sculpture will be the largest in the world.

Location and Address Crazy Horse Memorial, Avenue of the Chiefs, Crazy Horse, SD 57730. Telephone: (605) 673-4681.

Operating Hours 6:30 A.M. until dark during the summer; 8:00 A.M. until dark in the off-season.

Entrance Fees $7.00 per adult; under age 10 free; $17.00 per car. Special rates are provided for tours and other groups.

Exhibits and Events During the summer of 1998, the dedication of the face of Crazy Horse will be held as part of the 50th Anniversary observance that will commemorate the first blast on the mountain on June 3, 1948.

The annual Crazy Horse Volksmarch, a 6.2-mile hike, is held one weekend every June, and is the only time the public has access to the mountain while it is being carved. During the rest of the year, visitors observe the monument from three-quarters of a mile away.

Museum of the Plains Indians

Located in Browning, Montana, the museum showcases the cultures of the northern Plains tribes. The museum includes art exhibits and artifacts from the Blackfeet, Crow, Lakota, and Cheyenne.

Location and Address Museum of the Plains Indians, near the junction of Highways 2 and 89. P.O. Box 400, Browning, MO 59417. Telephone: (406) 338-2230.

Operating Hours Open 9 A.M.–5 P.M. June through September; and 10 A.M.–4:30 P.M. October to May.

Entrance Fees $4.00 per adult; children ages 6 to 12 $1.00; children under 6 free; groups of 10 or more $1.00 per person.

< 56 >

Black Kettle Museum and Battle of the Washita National Historic Site

Virtually ignored for more than a century, efforts are underway to make the site of the battle of the Washita in western Oklahoma a national monument. Nearby in the town of Cheyenne, a statue of a fleeing Indian woman and child stands in the courthouse entry as a tribute to those killed or left homeless by Custer's 1868 attack.

The Black Kettle Museum is maintained by the Oklahoma Historical Society.

Location and Address Black Kettle Museum, at the junction of U.S. Highway 283 and State Highway 47 in Cheyenne, Oklahoma. P.O. Box 252, Cheyenne, OK 73628. Telephone: (405) 497-3929.

Operating Hours Open 9 A.M.–5 P.M. Wednesday through Saturday; and 1 P.M.–5 P.M. Sundays in the winter.

Entrance Fees Admission is free.

Exhibits and Events The museum collection includes Indian and Seventh Cavalry artifacts from the battle of the Washita period.

Fort Fetterman State Historic Site

General George Crook marched out of Fort Fetterman in the spring of 1876 to look for the Sioux and Cheyenne led by Sitting Bull and Crazy Horse. He found them on June 17, 1876, along the banks of Rosebud Creek in southern Montana. The one-day battle that followed took Crook's men out of action for weeks. (The fort was named for Lieutenant William J. Fetterman, whose entire 81-man detachment was wiped out during the Powder River War.)

Today, Fort Fetterman, located about seven miles northwest of Douglas, Wyoming, is a state historic site. A few original buildings, one of them housing a museum, still stand.

Location and Address Fort Fetterman State Historic Site, 752 Highway 93, Douglas, WY 82633. Telephone: (307) 358-2864.

< 57 >

Operating Hours Open 9 A.M.–5 P.M. in the summer.
Entrance Fees Admission is free.
Exhibits and Events The museum displays artifacts from the fort's days as an infantry outpost during the Sioux campaign, and from the period when the fort served as a stockade.

Fort Robinson State Park

Located in the Nebraska Panhandle, the site of Crazy Horse's death is surrounded by 22,000 of some of the wildest acres left on the high Plains. Living history demonstrations give visitors a glimpse of life in the time of Custer, Crazy Horse, and Sitting Bull.

Location and Address Fort Robinson State Park, P.O. Box 392, Crawford, NE 69339. Telephone: (308) 665-2900.
Operating Hours Open 8 A.M.–5 P.M. Memorial Day to Labor Day, Monday through Saturday; and 9 A.M.–5 P.M. Sunday.
Entrance Fees $2.50 per vehicle.
Exhibits and Events Battle reenactments and other dramatic events are presented throughout the summer.

Sand Creek Massacre Site

Located north of Chivington, Colorado, a marker is the sole reminder of the murder of hundreds of peaceful Indians by overzealous volunteers under Colonel John Chivington.

Wounded Knee Massacre Site

Located just east of Wounded Knee, South Dakota, on the Pine Ridge Reservation, a plain stone marker memorializes the 200 Lakota killed by men of the Seventh Cavalry on December 29, 1890. The massacre was considered a national scandal even then. It was the last time Indians and white men met in pitched battle.

CHRONOLOGY OF THE INDIAN WARS

1600s	Wars with the Ojibwa and Sioux push the Cheyenne from central Minnesota onto the Plains.
1770s	The Lakota Sioux join the Cheyenne on the northern Plains.
1854	Grattan Incident near Fort Laramie ends uneasy truce between southern Lakota and the United States.
1864	Sand Creek massacre
1866	Powder River War begins.
1867	Seventh Cavalry organized. George Armstrong Custer named lieutenant colonel.
1868	Treaty of 1868. Army closes Powder River forts; U.S. establishes Great Sioux Reservation in the Dakota Territory and gives Indians hunting rights in unceded territory.
	Seventh Cavalry under Custer attacks Black Kettle's village in the battle of the Washita.
1872	Sitting Bull and Crazy Horse lead resistance to construction of Northern Pacific Railroad in Yellowstone River valley.
1873	Custer leads Northern Pacific Railroad escort, defeats Indians under Sitting Bull on August 4 and August 12.
1874	Custer's Black Hills expedition
1875	U.S. government demands that Sitting Bull and his followers go to the reservation.
January 1876	Indians ignore the government's order to go to the reservation.

< 59 >

May 1876	Gibbon's Crow scouts spot Sitting Bull's camp.
June 17, 1876	Battle of the Rosebud
June 25, 1876	Custer's Crow and Arikara scouts spot Sitting Bull's village.
	Battle of the Little Bighorn
September 1876	Battle of Slim Buttes
	Reservation Sioux cede Black Hills to U.S. government.
November 1876	Village of Dull Knife destroyed.
September 5, 1877	Crazy Horse killed.
December 15, 1890	Sitting Bull killed.
December 29, 1890	Battle of Wounded Knee

FURTHER READING

Bachrach, Deborah. *Custer's Last Stand: Opposing Viewpoints*. San Diego: Greenhaven Press, 1990.

Bodow, Steven. *Sitting Bull: Sioux Leader*. Austin, TX: Raintree Steck-Vaughn, 1992.

Bonvillain, Nancy. *The Teton Sioux*. New York: Chelsea House, 1994.

_____. *The Cheyennes: People of the Plains*. Brookfield, CT: Millbrook Press, 1996.

Ferrell, Nancy Warren. *The Battle of the Little Bighorn in American History*. Springfield, NJ: Enslow, 1996.

Freedman, Russell. *The Life and Death of Crazy Horse*. New York: Holiday House, 1996.

Reedstrom, E. Lisle. *Custer's Seventh Cavalry: From Fort Riley to the Little Bighorn*. New York: Sterling, 1992.

WEB SITES

For basic information on the Little Bighorn Battlefield National Monument, go to:
http://www.nps.gov/pub_aff/bigh.htm

For up-to-date information on all National Park Service parks and links to related sites, go to:
http://www.nps.gov

To learn about the National Museum of the American Indian, the Smithsonian's newest addition, go to:
http://www.si.edu/organiza/museums/nmah/start.htm

Administered by the Bismarck, North Dakota, *Tribune*, the Voices from the Little Bighorn site offers a wealth of information. Go to:
http://www.ndonline.com/tribwebpage/oldwest/littlebighorn/ *bighorn.html

The National Register of Historic Places is a good resource for finding preserved sites related to the battle. Go to:
http://www.cr.nps.gov/nr/home.html

SOURCE NOTES

Part One

1. Quoted in Robert Utley, *The Lance and the Shield: The Life and Times of Sitting Bull* (New York: Henry Holt & Company, 1993), p. 247.

2. Edward S. Godfrey, "Custer's Last Battle," *Century*, January 1892, reprinted in *The Custer Reader*, Paul Andrew Hutton, ed. (Lincoln, NE: University of Nebraska Press, 1992), p. 269.

3. Quoted in Utley, *The Lance and the Shield*, p. 250.

4. Ibid., p. 214.

< 61 >

5. Wooden Leg and Thomas B. Marquis, *Wooden Leg: A Warrior Who Fought Custer* (Lincoln, NE: University of Nebraska Press, 1931), p. 383.

6. Quoted in Evan S. Connell, *Son of the Morning Star: Custer and the Little Bighorn* (San Francisco: North Point Press, 1984), p. 242.

Part Two

1. Wooden Leg and Marquis, *Wooden Leg: A Warrior Who Fought Custer*, p. 202.

2. Quoted in Connell, *Son of the Morning Star*, p. 11.

3. Ibid., p. 234.

4. Quoted in Angie Debo, *A History of the Indians of the United States* (Norman, OK: University of Oklahoma Press, 1970), p. 259.

5. Wooden Leg and Marquis, *Wooden Leg: A Warrior Who Fought Custer*, p. 200.

6. Godfrey, "Custer's Last Battle," p. 277.

7. Quoted in Robert Utley, *Frontier Regulars: The United States Army and the Indian, 1866–1891* (New York: Macmillan Publishing Co., 1984), p. 257.

8. Robert Utley, *Cavalier in Buckskin: George Armstrong Custer and the Western Military Frontier* (Norman, OK: University of Oklahoma Press, 1988), p. 188.

9. Quoted in Connell, *Son of the Morning Star*, p. 204.

10. Quoted in Utley, *Cavalier in Buckskin*, p. 16.

11. Ibid., p. 34.

12. Quoted in New York *Herald*, July 7, 1876, reprinted in *The Custer Reader*, p. 387.

13. Godfrey, "Custer's Last Battle," p. 277.

14. Quoted in Utley, *Frontier Regulars*, p. 257.

< 62 >

15. Jerome A. Greene, ed., *Lakota and Cheyenne: Indian Views of the Great Sioux War, 1876–77* (Norman, OK: University of Oklahoma Press, 1994), pp. 42–43.

16. Quoted in Stephen E. Ambrose, *Crazy Horse and Custer* (Garden City, NY: Doubleday & Company, 1975), p. 436.

17. Quoted in Connell, *Son of the Morning Star*, p. 10.

18. Greene, ed., *Lakota and Cheyenne*, pp. 44–45.

19. Quoted in Connell, *Son of the Morning Star*, p. 279.

20. Reprinted in Ibid., p. 278.

21. Quoted in Utley, *Cavalier in Buckskin*, p. 188.

22. Ibid.

23. Quoted in Ambrose, *Crazy Horse and Custer*, p. 134.

24. Ibid., p. 134.

25. Quoted in Alvin M. Josephy Jr., *500 Nations: An Illustrated History of North American Indians* (New York: Alfred A. Knopf, 1994), p. 406.

Part Three

1. Quoted on National Park Service website: **http://www.nps.gov**

OTHER SOURCES

Bodow, Steven. *Sitting Bull.* Austin, TX: Raintree Steck-Vaughn, 1994.

Brown, Dee. *Bury My Heart at Wounded Knee: An Indian History of the American West.* New York: Holt, Rinehart, and Winston, 1970.

Fellman, Michael. *Citizen Sherman: A Life of William Tecumseh Sherman.* New York: Random House, 1995.

Foner, Eric and John A. Garraty. *The Reader's Companion to American History.* Boston: Houghton Mifflin, 1991.

Greene, Jerome A., ed. *Battles and Skirmishes of the Great Sioux War,*

< 63 >

1876–1877: The Military View. Norman, OK: University of Oklahoma Press, 1993.

Johnson, Michael. *The Native Tribes of North America.* London: Windrow & Greene, Ltd., 1993.

Lazarus, Edward. *Black Hills, White Justice.* New York: HarperCollins, 1991.

Michino, Gregory. *The Mystery of E Troop: Custer's Gray Horse Company at the Little Bighorn.* Missoula, MT: Mountain Press Publishing Co., 1994.

Morris Jr., Roy. *Sheridan: The Life and Wars of General Phil Sheridan.* New York: Vintage Books, 1992.

Sandoz, Mari. *Crazy Horse: The Strange Man of the Oglalas.* Lincoln, NE: The University of Nebraska Press, 1992.

Scott, Douglas D., Richard A. Fox Jr., Mellisa A. Connor, and Dick Harman. *Archaeological Perspectives on the Battle of the Little Bighorn.* Norman, OK: University of Oklahoma Press, 1989.

Waldman, Carl. *Atlas of the North American Indians.* New York: Facts On File, 1985.

Welch, James. *Killing Custer.* New York: W. W. Norton, 1994.

INDEX